Write that Book Now!

Julia A. Royston

BK Royston Publishing
Jeffersonville, IN
502-802-5385
http://www.bkroystonpublishing.com
bkroystonpublishing@gmail.com

© Copyright – 2016

All Rights Reserved. No part of this book may be reproduced, stored in a retrieval system, or transmitted by any means without the written permission of the author.

Cover Design: Vikiana

ISBN-13:978-1-946111-00-5
ISBN-10:1-946111-00-7

Printed in the United States of America

Dedication

I dedicate this book to anyone who has ever dreamed of writing a book, wanted to write a book or is currently writing a book. This book is for you!

Acknowledgement

First, I acknowledge my Lord and Savior Jesus Christ for giving me all of my gifts and especially my gift to write His words.

My husband who is always supportive, loving and encouraging me to utilize all of my gifts and talents. Thank you, honey.

To my mother, Dr. Daisy Foree, who is my number one cheerleader and always tells me, "hang in there, you can do it." To my father, Dr. Jack Foree, who is never far away from me in my spirit or heart. I only have to look in the mirror each day to see him.

To Rev. Claude and Mrs. Lillie Royston who support me in everything I do. Especially, Rev. Royston for his careful eye to detail and his sensitive heart to content.

To the rest of my family, I love you and thank you for your prayers, support and love.

To my great friend Vanessa Collins who told me to write this book years ago. Thanks for being there with me every step of the way. Love you.

Julia Royston

Table of Contents

Dedication	Iii
Acknowledgements	Iv
Introduction	ix
Why Do You Want to Write a Book?	1
The Topic	3
The Message of the Book	5
The Outline	7
Writing the Manuscript	11
Writing is Emotional	15
Look for Opposition	17
Rough Draft	19
Re-writes	21
Finish the Book!	23
Do You Need a Coach/Mentor?	25

Writing Conferences, Retreats and Workshops	29
Think like a boss	31
Submit Your Final Draft	33
Initial Strategic Planning Guide to Market and Promote of Your Book	35
About the Author	41
More Books By This Author	43

Introduction

So you've always wanted to write a book? Of course, you have! I have written more than 30 books and excited to share my tips, tricks and talent with you on writing your first of many books.

Now, before we get started, let me tell you that my company is here to help you complete and not just to start your book.

If you get stuck, have a problem or a question related to writing a book, don't hesitate to reach out to me and schedule a conversation at www.talkwithroyston.com. We'll be happy to help.

For information regarding the Write. Publish. Promote Series from Julia Royston, visit: Http://www.juliaroystonstore.com

We have wasted enough time dreaming, hoping and believing to be a published author. Turn the page to get started and definitely "Write that Book Now!"

Julia Royston

Why Do You Want to Write a Book?

So, you've always wanted to write a book? Of course, you have! First, think, why do you want to write a book? What do you want to say? Do you know something about that topic? What are you passionate about? These are just a few of the questions that you need to ask yourself before writing a book. Now, if you answered yes to the first question then that's good! Now to the second question, if you have an idea of why you want to write then that's great! If you said yes to the third question, and you know exactly what you want to say in your book then that's Fantastic! You are well on your way to becoming a published author.

But, if you answered that you want to write but you don't know what to write or what to say, then I have a few suggestions for you. Don't give up on your dream of being a published author. You just have to put in a little more time to get to the topic so, let's find a topic.

The Topic

If you don't have a topic to write about then, let's find one. Go to Google and type in "Bestselling books." Find a list of the bestselling books that are currently on the market. This list will help you determine what books people are actually buying. If one of the topics interests you then, decide to write about it. Don't worry about the title or how long your book will be compared to the book that is already published. At this point, we are just trying to determine the topic. You also want to distinguish your book from the books that are out there so, if you decide on a particular popular topic then determine a different angle or approach to the topic.

Also, I caution you to write about a topic that you have a genuine interest in. Remember that once your book is published, you will have to speak about your book as well as remember the title and where to buy it. On the other hand, if the topic you want to write about is a topic on the bestsellers list, you are well on your way to writing a book that not only people want to read but are willing to buy. Once you have decided on a topic, it is now time to begin the writing process.

Over the years, I have developed my own approach to writing books. I have written books purely from inspiration, having an outline with the issues I want to discuss in the book clearly detailed.

My first suggestion is to approach your book with the way that works best for you. If it's not broke, don't fix it. If you get stuck and need help, reach out to a writing coach or someone who has written books before.

For first time authors, I suggest having an outline with the subjects that you want to cover so that it helps with writer's block and the flow of your writing.

The Message of the Book

The message of the book and the topic of the book are different. The topic of the book is what you want to write about or the genre of the book. Fiction or romance fiction or self-help for domestic violence or even how to fix a sink. These are just some sample topics for a book. Inside the general topic of the book should be a message that you want to deliver to the reader. For example, the topic of the book is "Six Ways to Fix a Sink." The message of the book is that anybody can fix a sink with these simple instructions, step by step images and/or an instructional DVD. In other words, the message of the book should be related to the why of the book or the what? Remember that at the end of a speech, talk, lesson or instruction, there should be a reason why you did the talk, taught the lesson or gave the instructions. Why? The message of the book should be that why, or the reason for the book being written in the first place. Think about the reason or message of your book. It should connect with you first because you have to be passionate about and believe in what you are writing. Secondly, there should be someone else in the world who needs that message right now. The reason for my writing this book, "Write that Book, Now" is because there are billions of people in the world with many diverse needs, problems and situations. Your story, message and book could help them with that problem or situation. That's my message to you, "Write that Book Now!" Let's go!

The Outline

The outline should cover the topics that you want to discuss in your book. It's plain and simple. The topics do not have to be in final order or level of importance. The importance of the outline is to have a focus for the book, and if there are more issues surrounding the topic that are not included in the first outline then those issues could be for future books. Your book needs to have a focused topic, but under that topic should be the points or message that you wish to deliver. These should all be the determined in the outline.

You can write down the outline on paper. Others have suggested putting each topic on a note card. I sit down at a computer and begin writing my outline. Each line of my document should point to the one topic that I want to discuss.

For example, if your book was about 10 ways to be happy, the outline could look like the following:

Topic: 10 Ways to Be Happy

Happiness Definition

Life

Family

Health

Success

Business

Freedom

Now, before I give someone an idea for a best-selling book, I will stop at the above list of potential topics. The outline above is not in a particular order but clearly lists the topics that I, the author, would deem important, in my opinion, for happiness. With this outline, underneath each topic, begin writing about the topics on the outline. So, first, what is the definition of happiness? Second, what about your life would bring happiness? Third, what about family could or would make you happy?

You are writing your book based on the outline and filling in the blanks of the text under each topic. It's just that simple.

An outline is a great guide and map to writing your book. Once you are finished filling in the blanks or writing the text under your outline topics, go back and read what you have written. It will surprise you how much you have written. These topics can now be transposed into chapter titles. You could leave the chapter titles as simple one-word headings or adjust them to longer sentences. It is your choice.

Writing the Manuscript

You have the outline and should begin writing the manuscript immediately once the outline is developed and determined. If you are like me, you enjoy writing and don't find it hard to find the time or effort to write. Everyone is not the same and it may be your first book and your first attempt at writing a book. Here are some helpful hints for writing your book.

Schedule Time

Schedule time to write each day. Look at your weekly schedule. Determine when you get up, have to be at work and what your evenings look like. When do you have the most time to write? Is it in the morning when you wake up or in the evening before you go to bed? If I am focused on a topic, I write whenever I have free time, morning, noon and night. For you and your life, it might not be that easy. You decide but get to a time, schedule each day and stick to it. The book won't write itself so, you have to approach it like any other task. Make time for it. You make time for everything else and this is no different.

It has been suggested that you write for periods of time and then take breaks. These breaks cause you to walk away from the manuscript, rest your mind and body so that you can be more productive when you return to your manuscript. However, you do it, just do it. Write until you finish the book. The bottom line of finishing the book is to write.

Get an accountability partner

Tell someone that you are writing a book and let them hold you accountable for it. Get out your calendar and schedule times and days to check in with this person. Tell them your frustrations and possible delays in getting the book done. Let them motivate you and help you get the book done. You may even have to reach out to a professional book writing coach or mentor to help you stay committed to the process. That's what Julia

Royston Enterprises does. They help authors get started and keep moving forward until they achieve the end result of being a published author. Reach out to someone who has actually written a book. They know the process intimately and can offer suggestions to help you keep going until you finish. No matter how long it takes, keep going until you finish. There is someone waiting on your book. Don't stop until you are done!

Commitment and Determination

As with any undertaking, there must be a level of commitment, determination and dedication to getting it done. There should be a sense of pride, courage, wisdom and faith in what you are attempting. No matter what that project is there will be distractions, physical tiredness, possible writer's block, family crisis and financial delays but be determined to get it done. I've had writers reach out to me who have wanted to publish a book for more than 40 years. I know why they haven't done it yet and that's because they weren't committed to doing it in the past but because so much time has passed, they now realize that they don't know how much longer they will live, so they are more focused now than ever. Put in the work, stay committed to anything and you will reap the rewards for your efforts.

Writing is Emotional

Your thoughts, feelings, pain, joys and experiences can and may be included in your book. Time after time, I have had authors tell me of the emotional roller coaster ride that they have been on while writing their book. The autobiographical genre brings out the hidden, deep, dark and sometimes extremely painful experiences in a person's life. I have had authors stop writing because they didn't want to face the past. But, I have encouraged them that they can't overcome what they won't face. Some of you might ask, I thought she was a publisher? I am, but writing is emotional. Writing brings up emotions and situations from the past that you thought you had conquered, only to have them be revisited and realize that the pain hasn't fully gone away. Remember that someone else has and is experiencing that same pain. Your ability to live past your pain could be a message that someone needs to hear so that they can get past theirs as well.

Writing is therapeutic and directly tied to your emotional well-being. Writer, heal thyself through your writing. Keep writing.

Look for Opposition

In addition to the emotional impact that writing will have on you, the people around you will suddenly feel some way about you writing a book. Look for the opposition, jealousy, doubt and fear to come from someone close to you. I have written close to 30 books myself, helped more than 35 authors publish their books and coached countless others in writing their books, and it happens every time. Everyone is not going to be happy that you are achieving your goal of writing a book. You, who are reading this book, will experience the same thing. The majority of the time, the person will be someone closest to you. I caution you to just be ready for it. If the person doesn't reveal themselves while you are writing the book, they will reveal themselves after it is published, the book is on a book shelf somewhere or you are selling it out of the back of your car. Jealousy, envy and sudden distance will occur from someone. It happens every single time. On the other hand, there will be celebration, motivation, support and sales from people you didn't think would support or celebrate you so, look for that as well. It will surprise you who your true friends are and what family members have been jealous of you all of your lives but you didn't know it. Don't say I didn't warn you.

Rough Draft

Once you have a finished filling in the text under your outline items, then you have completed the rough draft.

Congratulations! Yippee! You have finished the first draft of your book. There may be more drafts to come but celebrate the first rough draft.

After you have finished the rough draft, put it away for at least three days. Don't look at it, review it or do any re-writing for these three days. You need time away from the book so that you can give it a fresh approach when you re-read what you wrote.

Three days after you finished the first rough draft, open the document or open the journal and read what you wrote. Read it out loud so that you can hear exactly how the book sounds to your ears through your voice. Don't edit yet, just read it all of the way through. Don't delete anything. Don't cross out anything and please, don't throw away anything! Just read it. Feel the passion in the words. Hear the emotion in your voice. Just read it. Put it away again and think about what you just wrote first. Don't jump right in at first but meditate on what you just wrote. How did it make you feel? How did it sound to you? What do you think that you left out? What do you want to add? Just think about the book first.

A couple of days later, open the document or open the journal and begin going line by line, reading it out loud again and making changes. This is called the re-write phase of writing the book.

Re-Writes

Re-writing is a critical phase after the first draft and should be seen with fresh eyes after the rough draft is finished. I find that reading a manuscript after I have put it away for a few days really allows me to be ready to do the re-writes. In the re-writes, your focus is to not start the book from scratch but to add any missing pieces or any other things that you want to say. Don't remove anything unless it does not follow the outline or isn't pertinent to the book. Don't delete it permanently because it could be the idea or important piece to another book but shouldn't be included in this first book. When you are finished with the re-writes, let it go to someone else. Let someone you trust read it to make sure that it makes sense to them and the message you were trying to get across was delivered. If not clear, ask them what was not clear and make the change. It is that simple. Just make the message clearer, don't delete or throw away the book. Criticism comes with the territory of writing. Don't let your emotions stop or block you from creating and delivering the best book possible. You put your feelings into the book but don't let your feelings stop you from moving forward to finish the book. I am the first to admit that I am sensitive about everything I create and want people to like it as much as I do, but at the end of the day, people still have to be able to understand what you wrote even if they don't agree. That is the beauty of writing, it is not that people have to agree, but they do have to understand and get the clear picture of what you were trying to say in the book. There are books out there that are very controversial and do well selling in the marketplace. But a poorly written book is just that, a poorly written book, no matter the topic.

Finish the Book!

Whether on a napkin, paper, tissue, computer or journal notebook, just write. No matter when you write, just write. There is no other way around it, just write and finish the book.

No matter how long it takes or what you need to finish, just finish it. Whether it takes six months or six years, finish the book.

Get the heart of a finisher and finish the book. There is nothing like finishing any project but when your book is finished, published and it is available online or on a book shelf, there is nothing like it.

Don't wait another minute! Don't delay another day! Write and Finish!

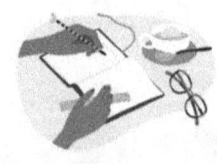

Do You Need a Coach/Mentor?

If you get stuck, get a coach, mentor or accountability partner to help you finish your book. Don't leave notebooks lying around for years without finishing your book. Get some help. There are plenty of writing coaches, coaching programs and free online tutorials to help you finish your book.

Visit www.talkwithroyston.com to schedule a conversation and get the help you need to finish your book.

Sacrifice and Invest in Your Dream

To purchase a pair of shoes, dress, car or vacation, you make the sacrifices necessary to make that dream a reality. Writing a book is no different. You will have to make the sacrifice of your time, money and effort to make that dream of being a published author a reality.

There will be an investment that will have to be made when becoming a published author. Some of you may have to buy or upgrade your technology such as your phone or computer to make sure that you have all of the tools you need to write your book correctly. All published books have to be in an electronic form before the publishing process can continue. Do you have the technology skills and equipment to make that happen? You may not now, but it can happen. Go to the store, ask the questions, look into your budget and make that sacrifice and investment into your dream of being a published author.

You may need a coach to help and guide you while writing your book. Coaching is not free. Be prepared for the investment into writing coaching. Ask up front exactly how much each session will cost. Will there be a reduced fee if multiple sessions are purchased or is there a flat rate for each coaching session? How long will each session last and is the coach available for consultation in between sessions? In other words, can you reach out to the coach via email, text or phone in between sessions?

That is an important question to ask the coach before signing on the dotted line of the agreement or making the first payment.

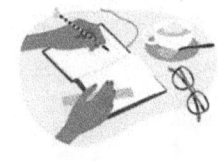

Writing Conferences, Retreats and Workshops

If you are serious about your writing journey before and even after becoming a published author, I suggest that you attend at least one writing conference, retreat or workshop. I host and attend a writing conference every year. These conferences offer opportunities to learn, network with other authors and publishers as well as receive guidance and possible critique of your writing. These opportunities and many others can be found at writing conferences, retreats or workshops.

There is a wide range of costs for these conferences so read the fine print for what is actually being offered during the conference. The fees can range from tens of dollars to several thousand. There may be a local or regional writing conference close by so look in your area. Your public library or writing department at your local college or university should be able to help you find a writing course or conference in your area. There are several national and international conferences held in exotic places and sites so, do your homework. In the past, there have been publishers who are looking for authors to sign to their publishing company and will review, critique and comment on your works for free. Publishers have nothing to review if you have not written anything, so write as much as possible. Outline the manuscript and have at least one chapter to be reviewed. The publishers are looking at the quality of your writing, the subject matter that you write about compared to the demand and sales potential for this particular market for this book's subject.

I encourage you to have at least a chapter written in your book prior to attending these conferences to be able to obtain a writing critique. There may be an additional cost for the critique but it is worth it.

Think Like a Boss

As stated previously, writing is a business. Take the business of writing seriously. Do your homework by conducting your own research. Ask as many questions as you feel comfortable with asking. If the person you are seeking to do business with doesn't answer your questions, move on to someone else. A book is like a baby, would you hand over your newborn child to just anyone? No, so, don't hand over your book to just anyone. It's precious to you so, make sure that the publisher you sign a contract with treats your manuscript like the precious baby it is.

Submit Your Final Draft

Once you have finished your rough draft, done the re-writes and had someone else has review your book who thinks it is good then, it will be time to submit your final draft to be considered for publishing.

Your book should be typed using a word processing software such as Microsoft Word. You can also use the Google Drive word processing software or Open Office word processing program to allow you to type your document. Your manuscript should have a 12-point font, preferably Times New Roman and not a script font because it will be changed immediately to a more readable font.

The manuscript should be double spaced and with a one-inch margin around the entire document. The one-inch margin should be for the top, bottom, left and right margins.

If you would like for BK Royston Publishing, LLC to review or publish your book, go to www.talkwithroyston.com to schedule a conversation with a member of the BK Royston Publishing Team.

If you are interested in self-publishing your book, obtain my book, "Publish that Book Now" by Julia A. Royston at www.juliaroystonstore.com.

We are excited for each of you on your journey to being a published author. If you need help, reach out to us, but for now, Let's go and Write That Book, Now!

Initial Strategic Planning Guide to Market and Promote of Your Book

You have completed the rough draft of your book and possibly submitted it to a publishing company. This is awesome, but you need to begin to strategize how you will sell and market your book.

Some will ask, isn't this too early? My book isn't even finished yet? I don't know the title or have a cover? That is fine because in the next few pages we will map out a plan to market the book based on the topic alone.

It is never too early to be prepared to promote your book and to receive the possible sales of your book.

The next few pages are just a planning guide to get your mind, body and team prepared for the upcoming best-selling book. You don't have a team yet? Well, we are here to help you formulate a team to get this book promoted and sold.

What is the topic or subject of your Book? For example: Inspirational/Self-Help book about Relationships

List the top five best-selling authors in this genre or topic. You will probably have to do your homework and look up the bestsellers on Amazon, New York Times Bestseller list, etc.

What is the message of your book? The message of your book could be different from the topic. For example, the topic of the book may be about relationships and titled, "Domestic Violence: He thought he had me!" The message of your book may be, ways to get out of a domestic violence situation. Another message could be ways to spot an abusive partner as well as ways to not get into the situation.

Name at least 3 Take a Ways/Hook - A take-away or a hook for your book is a point, issue, concept or information that you want the reader to remember. These take-aways or hook points can be the basis for talks, workshops or conferences about your book. Keep these handy for when any media outlet interviews you about your book.

What is the Target Date that you desire to have your book on the market? If you don't have a date, what is the best season for your book?

_____
_____
_____
_____
_____
_____
_____
_____

What is your scheduled time to write each day? If you enjoy writing in the early mornings, then other times of the day should be spent marketing and promoting.

Morning

Noon

Night

Early Morning

Who is your book's target audience? (Note: remember that you may target an audience with a book that does not appeal to that particular audience. This is a huge mistake for new authors. For example, if your market or target audience is men, make sure that the book's concept or idea, cover, interior vocabulary and marketing strategy is attractive to men.)

Men

Women

Young People

Children

Elderly

What social media outlets do you actively participate in?

Facebook

Twitter

Instagram

Periscope

BLAB

Pinterest

LinkedIN

Google PLUS

Do you have a website?

Yes

No

Have you ever attended a writing workshop?

No

Yes

If not, go to Google and search for writing workshops that are held in the area where you live.

List at least 50 people you believe would buy a book whom you would write. This list can be used later if you are able to compile a list of 50 people. If you cannot compile a list of at least 50 people, you need to expand your scope of influence in person and online.

About the Author

Julia Royston spends her days doing what she loves, writing, publishing, speaking about her why and motto, "Helping You Get Your Message to the Masses, Turn Your Words into Wealth and Be a Book Business Boss." Julia is the author of 140+ books, published 400+, recorded 3 music CDs and coached others to be published authors and business owners. She is the owner of five companies, a non-profit organization and the editor of the Book Business Boss Magazine.

To stay connected with Julia, visit www.juliaakroyston.com.

Social Media

Facebook, Instagram, LinkedIN, TikTok and Threads - @juliaaroyston

X - @juliaakroyston

Get the Entire Write. Publish. Promote Series Today by visiting: http://www.juliaroystonstore.com

More Books By This Author

www.ingramcontent.com/pod-product-compliance
Lightning Source LLC
Chambersburg PA
CBHW071231160426
43196CB00012B/2481